Norwich Cathedral

A SHORT GUIDE
by Alan Webster M.A., B.D.
Dean of St Paul's

Published by the Dean and Chapter 1984

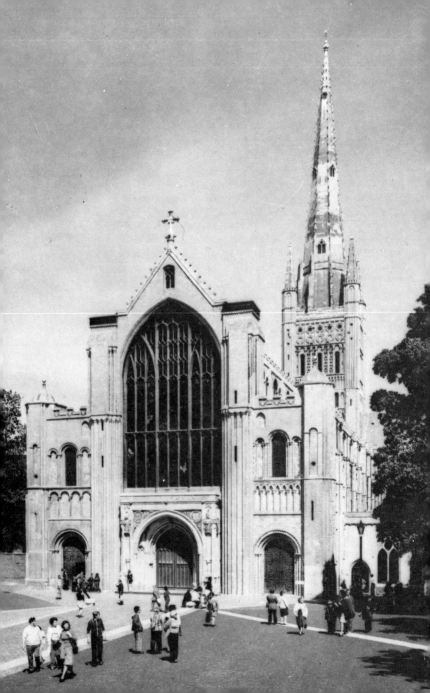

What is it for?

You can appreciate a great cathedral without detailed knowledge of its history, architecture or religious traditions, but you need to understand why it was built and what purpose it fulfils today.

Norwich Cathedral has always been the home of a community with religious purposes, worship, study, teaching and charitable work, serving the city of Norwich and the surrounding countryside, with its towns and villages. For the first 400 years the community was twofold: monks and their supporters, and the Bishop and his supporters. The monastery was suppressed at the Reformation but the cathedral continued its work.

Today it is the home of a Christian community which has the task of expressing and spreading the faith, the hope and the love which they believe are mirrored in the life and death and resurrection of Jesus Christ. It is designed to burn into our minds the fact that human beings need to worship and to pray, to devote time and attention to each other and to God, and give priority in their lives to love and service, wonder and reverence, sympathy and self-sacrifice. It contains the seat (Greek *cathedra* – a chair) of the Bishop, which symbolises his work of teaching, administration and 'chairing' the work of the Church, carried on by a team, lay and ordained, who see the cathedral as a reinforcement point.

Here then is a great building, the achievement of many generations, which expresses changing ideals and beliefs about religion and community, philosophy and art, heaven and hell. No one can sympathise with *all* these ideals and beliefs; some may even repel you, but somewhere or other within such a comprehensive and surprising building everyone finds something to stir his imagination. If you give some time to reflect, and if possible to be still and meditate, this cathedral can be a momentary monastery for you in the twentieth century.

3

Prayer has been offered here for nearly 900 years, and today worship and prayer, teaching and thought, friendship and care, music and drama all find a home in it. Be assured that you are welcome here and that this cathedral is *your* cathedral as much as if you came as a visitor or pilgrim in the first centuries of its life. Here prayer and reflection can result in a fresh concern for vagrants in Norwich, seen in the opening of the Night Shelter in St Martin at Oak, a redundant church, or the international ecumenical eucharist in 1973 to focus understanding of Julian of Norwich, a pioneer English mystic. Instead of an introverted Barchester or 'All gas and gaiters' we hope you may find quiet dynamism. Buildings, music and liturgy can speak when words lose their power.

Two misericords, lion and dragon fighting and monk reading

The maintenance of cathedrals is not the responsibility of the state, as in most continental countries, but of the Church itself. A sense of the value of the spiritual dimension binds together those who care about the life of Norwich Cathedral. Free Churchmen and Roman Catholics and other men of goodwill, in practice, help to maintain it. Whatever your religious allegiance or your agnosticism, this building can speak of perspectives we easily forget and lead us to a quiet hopefulness about human life. We hope you will find that you can, with integrity, share in its work and maintenance. Much depends for the future upon the attitudes of the younger generation: will they find support for their faith, idealism and life-styles within this great inheritance? The liveliness of the Young Friends of Norwich Cathedral suggests that some of them will say 'yes' to that question, and that the cathedral will not become a museum, or die like some dinosaur stranded from the age of Christendom, but continue to be the home of a lively community.

Welcome and Information

There are always people on duty, volunteers as well as staff, to welcome you, whether you come from Britain or abroad. The cathedral is opened each day at 7.30 a.m. and the first service of Morning Prayer is at 7.35 a.m.

The verger's office is under the organ screen.

The shop at the west end can help you with guide books in English, French, German, Spanish, Italian and Dutch.

Guides (with badges) and chaplains (in cassocks) are on duty in the summer. Please note that the guides and chaplains are volunteers and are embarrassed by tips.

A visitors' centre up the stairs outside the west end of the cathedral has an **exhibition** to enable you to find out as much as you can for yourself, and also a refreshment area with coffee, tea and lunch snacks.

Edith Cavell's grave is outside the south door, turn left.

At the busiest times the **Friends of the Cathedral** man an information table. Here you can join the Friends who help to maintain the cathedral.

There are **lavatories** under the stairs to the Visitors' Centre.

You should not hesitate to ask those who can tell you about the activities of the cathedral. You will find that there are services, discussions, holiday lectures, organ recitals and other music. The choir sings nearly every day. The clergy are always available and every Sunday the cathedral congregation welcomes visitors to coffee in the south transept after the 11 a.m. main morning service. There is a Sunday Club for children up to twelve during this service. All communicant members of any denomination are welcome to make their communion.

Naturally parishes are specially welcome at all services, and members of the Chapter and cathedral staff do their best to serve the churches in the city and county. Ministers of other denominations are equally welcome. Any who wish to arrange

Jesus
Chapel

their own services are asked to apply to the Cathedral Office.
Small chapels are readily available. The Sacrament is
reserved in St Andrew's Chapel. Members of the cathedral
staff have different specialisms and duties; theology, liturgy,
history, education, church music, industrial mission, pastoral
youth and social work, and as far as possible their time is at the
disposal of the diocese, other churches and visitors. The
cathedral seeks to be open and available to all comers, without
distinction of creed, class, colour or country.

Some History

Building began in 1096 as part of the programme of energetic, almost furious, construction initiated by the Normans after their conquest of Anglo-Saxon England in 1066. In western Europe between 1050 and 1350 there was a cathedral building boom, in which eighty cathedrals and thousands of churches were built. Norwich was the second or third largest city in the country, but in Saxon times not yet the centre of a diocese. The bishopric was moved from Thetford to be further away from the jurisdiction of Bury St Edmunds and into the city of Norwich where the conqueror had greater control than in the countryside. Herbert de Losinga, the first Bishop of Norwich, established his headquarters here in Norwich and obtained a large grant of land with the freedom from local control which he needed in order to establish and finance a Benedictine monastery for about fifty monks.

The site Losinga chose had already been used for burials (a pre-Norman skull was found in 1975) and earlier buildings were cleared. He had to provide accommodation not only for the cathedral and the monastery, but also for the diocesan structure, including his own palace, to the north of the cathedral and originally linked with it through a door in the nave. Today the foundations of his great house form the ground floor of the Old Palace building, a boarding house for Norwich School.

Losinga used Norfolk flints for the core of the building, but the fine white stone which gives Norwich its elegant finish came largely from Caen in Normandy, shipped across the Channel and up the Wensum through Yarmouth to Norwich, the end of the tidal section of the river. You can see a model of the ships in the Visitors' Centre exhibition. A short canal was constructed to link the cathedral with the river at Pull's Ferry in the Lower Close which lasted until well into the eighteenth century. The architect and planners and most of the craftsmen were Norman. In 1101 the cathedral was already in use and Herbert's successor, Bishop Eborard de Montgomery (1121–45), completed the work. The Norman work here has rounded arches, massive and secure; the pointed arches are Gothic, lighter and more graceful. Herbert de Losinga is always remembered on Founders Day, the Saturday nearest to 22 July, St Mary Magdalen's Day.

The magnificent vaulted roofs were added 300 years afterwards between 1465 and 1510, and the spire was built by Bishop James Goldwell (1472–99). Norwich is a Norman cathedral from the ground to the top of the tower, with late medieval roofs and spire.

At the Reformation the changes were very gradual – from the administrative point of view the Reformation was almost a non-event in Norwich. The monastery was dissolved in 1538 and its church became a 'New Foundation' cathedral, serving the city and the diocese. Community life slowly ground to a halt, though the choir continued. The school was refounded and developed. The last Prior became the first Dean. Former monks filled the residentiary canonries. One of the singing men, Osbert Parsley, whose monument can still be seen on the north side of the nave, sang at the daily offices from 1535 to 1585 through all the changes from Latin Mass to English Communion Service. Slowly the ideals of the Reformation were realised and Common Prayer in English was accepted as a reasonable, holy and lively form of worship.

In 1643, during the Civil War, the building was badly mauled by Puritan pillagers who identified it with the Royalist and Roman Catholic cause. All the crucifixes, brasses and windows and much else were destroyed. The town of Yarmouth even petitioned that it might use cathedral stone to build a new jetty, but this vandalism was resisted. The restoration from 1660 onwards was thorough and included the gift of new altar candlesticks from the city. Bishops, deans, canons and clergy returned to their duties. During the eighteenth century religious life in the diocese and the cathedral was quiet, uneventful and introverted, but from 1840 there were vigorous changes designed to meet the social and economic challenge of the Industrial Revolution. 'Barchester' attitudes were criticised. The laity and the clergy became more active. Large and widely representative congregations were encouraged to attend both regular and special services. The cathedral adopted new functions as a diocesan and civic church.

In the present century responsibility for the cathedral maintenance has largely passed from the clergy to the 5,000 Friends, who have been increasingly energetic. When more than sixty incendiary bombs fell on the roofs (1939–45) there were many willing helpers, including boys from Norwich School, who climbed the roofs to quench the flames. In 1975 the work of restoration was completed after the renewal of all the roofs as well as the radical strengthening of the spire and tower. A rolling programme of restoration now goes on year by year. The remaining monastic buildings have been adapted for contemporary needs, including music rooms for the choir, and the Visitors' Centre has been created in the ancient monastic guest quarters over the cloisters—a feature unique to Norwich. More than 500 volunteers assist in maintaining the life, welcome, and worship of the cathedral.

Effigy of Bishop
Herbert de Losinga

Itinerary of the Cathedral

The map attached to this guide suggests that the best route to walk round the cathedral is to **start at the west end of the nave**, under the great stained-glass window, and pause for an unrivalled view of the whole building. If you have entered by one of the other doors, it is worth walking the length of the nave and starting there. The brief tour which follows treats each part of the cathedral in turn.

Choir and Clergy

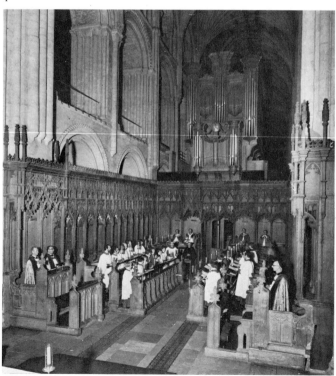

The Nave

The nave, which can seat 1,000, is regularly used for services for the diocese, the city, the county, youth organisations, old people's associations, church organisations and schools, and Christmas services of all kinds. It is also a fine setting for music and drama.

The nave is also used for exhibitions designed to remind us of contemporary tragedies and needs. The Norwich Third World Centre and Oxfam, both with their offices nearby, unite Christians, humanists and others in a common task. Here in the nave the Lord Mayor attends the Civic, Battle of Britain and Remembrance Services. Here is held a Careers Convention for school children every other year and exhibitions mounted by children in schools in the city and county.

The nave is dominated by the stone ribbed roof, with its marvellous bosses, recently repainted and relit, which were

Nave
clerestory

11

given by Bishop Lyhart (1446–72), using Robert Everard, an outstanding architect. The roof is a serene achievement – one of the most successful English vaults.

The bosses can be examined through the mirrors on wheels available for visitors; field glasses also help. The bosses are a strip cartoon of the whole story of God's involvement with man from creation to last judgement, as seen in the imagination of medieval Christians. The west seven bays, immediately over the west door, represent New Testament scenes, and the east seven, ending over the organ, Old Testament scenes. The main centre boss in each bay 'prefigures' the corresponding boss in the New Testament series; e.g. in the Old Testament series, Noah's Ark in the flood of water (a large boss clearly seen over the organ) 'prefigures' the New Testament boss, Christ's baptism in water. The prominent red-painted boss over the pulpit, representing Egyptians being drowned in the Red Sea, so that the Israelites can escape, 'prefigures' bosses in the New Testament series at the west end of the nave where Christ's

Nave bosses and *opposite*, Nave roof

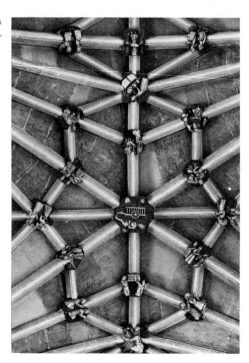

resurrection represents his escape from death, his final triumph over dark forces. The reasoning behind the arrangement of the bosses is that history repeats itself with a difference and God's work down the centuries can be detected. The circular hole in the roof, two feet across, was for lowering, on great feasts, a figure of an angel swinging a censer with incense, and for repairs and maintenance of the timbers which carried the external lead roof.

The window at the west end was built by Bishop Lyhart but was paid for out of the will of his predecessor, Bishop Alnwick (died 1449). The glass is Victorian (1854) given in memory of Bishop Stanley, and is much admired by Sir John Betjeman. In the upper sections it tells the story of the ascension of Christ and in the lower sections Moses leads the Israelites in the wilderness and sets up a serpent of brass on a pole in order to heal people who had been bitten by poisonous snakes. At the opposite end of the nave is the pulpitum or screen, also built by Lyhart, dividing the people's church (the nave) from the private church for the monks (the presbytery). The existing screen is largely a nineteenth-century copy of the original. Organs have been placed on this screen since the Middle Ages. The present organ, one of the largest in the country, was erected 1940–50, dividing the long vista from the west to the east end of the cathedral.

The nave is mercifully free of monuments, though the tributes to Bishop Stanley, who broke through 'Barchester' traditions (his son was Dean Stanley, thought to be portrayed in *Tom Brown's Schooldays*), and to Dean Willink, whose people's service filled the nave every Sunday evening, are reminders of a lively past. There are informative lists of bishops, deans and high stewards at the west end. The Bishop is the head of the diocese, the Dean, of the cathedral, and the High Steward is the leading lay adviser, a post vital for the well-being of Norwich Cathedral. On the vault in the south aisle, close to the pulpitum, notice three early medieval paintings of Herbert de Losinga offering a bribe to become Bishop, repenting, and building the cathedral. ('Losinga' is probably a place, but possibly derived from 'Losenger', a flatterer.) Close by is a grim example of sixteenth-century pop art: a skeleton, with far from accurate anatomy, warning the observer to remember his own death.

The two prominent Norman pillars with a spiral design, possibly prefabricated in the quarries at Caen, and similar to pillars at Durham, once carried a screen and were cut by its woodwork. A second pair of similar pillars form the core of

14

Nave
vault

other pillars as can be seen through the glass covering in the north aisle.

Even when the nave is crowded it is valuable to sit down, pause and look around. You may be able to detect carvings of a stag lying down in water, a pun or puzzle in stone (or rebus) on the name Lyhart, a modest 'signature' at the head of some of the pillars below the clerestory (the upper storey of the nave walls), above the triforium (the first storey above the nave). The later additions of the vaulted roof and the Perpendicular windows inserted at triforium level in the Norman walls which admit so much light from the broad East Anglian sky, harmonise remarkably with the earlier work.

The Choir

Passing under the organ screen notice the composition of the tower, presbytery, apse and light Perpendicular tracery, with flying buttresses outside – a triumph of design, generally considered one of the most glorious clerestories in England. The choir stalls, which originally extended across the crossing, were designed for the Benedictine monks with ten special stalls for the Bishop and other officials. The stalls and canopies have been frequently repaired but some date from Bishop Wakering (1416–25), and from Sir Thomas Erpingham, the commander of the English Archers at Agincourt (who also erected the gate bearing his name and effigy, opposite the west end of the Cathedral). The stalls have a remarkable series of misericords carved under the movable seats, probably so called from the Latin for 'mercy' as they supported the monks, tired when standing during long services.

You can see one of the misericords open on the north side, revealing an owl mobbed by small birds. Norfolk society has always been rural, fascinated by all kinds of living creatures, a country for ornithologists. Those who carved the birds and animals of Norwich revered life's wonders and praised their creator. In days when the medieval bestiary, or treatise on beasts, was popular the cathedral had the beginnings of an illustrated bestiary in stone and glass pointing to God's purpose for all created living things – the truth St Francis loved. You can find falcons in the choir stalls, a fox in the north ambulatory door carving, Julian's cat and even a kiwi in the regimental chapel windows. If you like dragons and frightening bugaboos, you should look at the cloister bosses. (Outside you can often see kestrels circling the spire and if you want to discover more of the marvellous life of the sea marshes and the Broads and the Breckland, call at the Norfolk Naturalists Trust at 72 The Close.)

Today, during term time, the choir sings God's praise twice on Sundays and once on most weekdays.

Recently the crossing has been cleared of pews to reveal the four piers which bear the tower and the spire, which were reinforced in 1964–5 when cracks appeared in the fabric. An altar has been placed under the tower so that the Holy Communion can be celebrated from a central point, enabling all those sitting in the four arms of the presbytery to see and hear and sing together, in response to the spirit of liturgical renewal which emphasises participation by all worshippers.

The lectern, dating from 1380, is 'a pelican in her piety' feeding her young (originally in a nest) from her own breast – a symbol of self-sacrifice. The design of the feathers on the wings is notable. It is Flemish, a sign of the close relations with the Low Countries. The lessons read at services are from modern translations, usually the New English Bible. The founder is buried under the seventeenth-century black marble slab in front of the high altar, with an aggressively Royalist and anti-Commonwealth inscription which replaced the ancient elaborate medieval tomb destroyed during the Civil Wars.

Behind and above the high altar two battered pieces of stone are all that remains of an ancient stone chair, perhaps brought from an earlier cathedral, at Thetford or Elmham, or even Dunwich. By putting it here the Normans continued the ancient Christian practice of seating the Bishop facing his people, like a Jewish teacher in synagogue or a Roman official in court. In 1974 medieval oak from the cathedral roof was used to construct the present wooden chair placed over the stones. Today the Bishop does not sit here but the chair is used to install each new bishop, and from this position he gives his blessing on great occasions.

On the south side of the presbytery notice the chantry tomb of Bishop Goldwell (1472–99), whose rebus, a gold well, can be seen above in the bosses of the roof. His effigy still has its original colours. Goldwell built the glorious spire (height 315 feet) – second only to Salisbury.

When Queen Elizabeth I visited Norwich Cathedral for a thanksgiving service, she was seated in the sanctuary opposite the tomb of her grandfather Sir William Boleyn which bears the Boleyn arms, a sad reminder of Anne Boleyn, her mother, who was executed by her father. It must have made her think! Queen Elizabeth II occupied the same position when she

Choir
looking west

Piers
of Tower

attended a thanksgiving service in April 1975 to celebrate the restoration of the cathedral. On this occasion the blessing was given jointly by Anglican, Free Church and Roman Catholic bishops and church leaders – a happy symbol of the fact that cathedrals are becoming centres of Christian unity, rather than the privileged possession of a particular denomination.

The Transepts

The transepts are large, seating about 200 people. Though the south transept is much restored, they are in all essentials Norman, with ribbed-roof vaulting constructed in 1510 by Bishop Nykke just before the Reformation. The carved monsters with little people in their mouths are a reminder that the primitive Christianity of the builders still had pagan elements. The transepts are used for the Sunday services and for the weekday Evensongs. The south transept is used for coffee for the congregation after the main Sunday morning service.

In the north transept notice **the chapel of St Andrew**, where the Sacrament is reserved. This quiet area, for private prayer and meditation, is enriched by the evocative Dutch painting by Jordaens the Younger, of Christ healing the woman with the issue of blood. The shepherd in the background piping to the sheep makes a charming scene. Parts of the window above date from a visit to Norwich by Cardinal Wolsey, and the statue is the work of John Skelton, a contemporary sculptor brought up in Norwich. Part of the floor has been cleared for those who prefer to pray without pews.

Literature about **Julian of Norwich**, the medieval mystic, is available in the pews. Her most famous discovery was the great affirmation wrung from her despite personal suffering, the Black Death and grim repression of Norfolk peasants, that, 'All shall be well, and all shall be well and all manner of things shall be well.' Various editions of her pioneering work, the first book in English by a woman, *Revelations of Divine Love*, are available in the shop and the bookstall, where there is also a map to help you if you wish to visit her cell in Carrow. If you are specially interested in Julian, the Cathedral Office has miscellaneous literature including the hymns and prayers used on 8th May, when she is always remembered.

The **north transept** has three intriguing statues illustrating episcopal attitudes during the last 200 years. Bishop Bathurst, carved by Chantry, on the left, meditates as in a long evening of reflection. Though very much in the 'Barchester' tradition, he steadily supported Catholic emancipation. He was also one of the two bishops who consistently voted for the Reform Bill in 1830–2. In the centre, the aristocratic and evangelical Bishop Pelham reclines at length. On the right, the statue of 'Sweet Vi' represents the young secretary of Bishop Pollock, a former headmaster who gave this marble tribute with its nosegay of romantic poetry. Beside Sweet Vi, notice the wall tablet with its restrained but moving inscription to George March, verger, 1640.

The door in **the south transept** into the ambulatory dates from the last Prior but one, Prior Robert Catton, whose initials can be seen on the fine medieval lock plate. The staircase in the west wall (not open to the public) gives access into the choir rooms, a boys' and men's vestry, a music library in memory of Brian Runnett (organist 1966–70), and the choir recreation room. The south wall of the south transept was entirely refaced by Salvin under Dean Pellew, in an unsympathetic heavy style to 'restore' this end of the cathedral and remove a fourteenth-century prison which had been inside the building – a necessary 'facility' when the Close 'administered' its own law and order, with the Dean as judge, jury and jailer!

To visit the grave of **Edith Cavell** (1865–1915) you should go out of the south door under the clock and turn left towards the east end of the cathedral, where her final words are inscribed on the wall: 'Standing as I do in view of God and eternity, I realise that patriotism is not enough. I must have no hatred or bitterness towards anyone.' Her simple grave is in 'Life's Green', the ancient burial place of the monks. Edith Cavell, like another English hero Horatio Nelson, was the child of a Norfolk parsonage. Prayers are said at her grave on Remembrance Sunday and her Bible with personal notes can be seen in the exhibition.

Ambulatory and Chapels

This section of the cathedral is used today for the 8 a.m. Holy Communion service each morning, preceded by Mattins said at 7.35 a.m. Here prayer for particular persons and causes, thanksgivings and meditations, as well as the reading of scripture in the services of Morning Prayer and Evening Prayer, continues throughout the year. Here lay people and the cathedral staff, lay and ordained, come in small groups every day to worship. The chapels round this processional way were originally built to enable those monks who were priests to say their daily individual mass.

A brief stroll round the ambulatory starting through Prior Catton's doorway in the south transept, brings you first to the **Bauchun Chapel of Our Lady of Pity**, given by the fourteenth-century corn storekeeper, with a good modern window telling the story of the Benedictine Order and its civilising work throughout Europe, given to commemorate Julian of Norwich – see the lowest right-hand panel. Enter through the screen. On your right is a painting of the moment when old Simeon held the Christ child, by John Opie (1761–1807). The chapel also contains a late medieval roof erected by William Sekyinton (1450) illustrating Chaucer's Man of Lawe's tale. The statue of Our Lady is by John Skelton. The screen, designed by Bernard Feilden, the cathedral architect, was made by Eric Stevenson of Wroxham, and the whole chapel was restored by the Friends of Norwich Cathedral in 1968.

The next chapel is called **St Luke's** and contains a battered medieval seven sacraments font. Starting from the west side by the wall, the sacraments illustrated are baptism, confirmation, penance, holy communion, marriage, ordination and extreme unction, with the crucifixion for the eighth side. You should spend time at the Despenser Reredos, the finest in the cathedral. A detailed description of this religious masterpiece dating from the generation which knew the Black Death and

MARTIN SCHWARD
Paris 1502

24

A view from the
north ambulatory
and *opposite*, Nativity
by Schwarz in the
Jesus Chapel

the visions of Julian of Norwich, will be found in the chapel. This chapel is used by the congregation of St Mary in the Marsh, whose church in the Close was demolished in 1570. In the ambulatory near by the chapel is the rugged effigy of an eleventh-century bishop which possibly represents Herbert de Losinga, with his hand raised in blessing. This effigy was originally outside the north transept.

St Saviour's Chapel, the Regimental Chapel of the Royal Norfolk Regiment, built in 1930, is on the site of the ruins of the Lady Chapel. The battle honours of the Norfolk Regiment, inscribed round the walls, form a miniature history of the rise of the British Empire. The chapel is used regularly by the Regiment and its successors.

The **Jesus Chapel**, skilfully restored by Stephen Dykes Bower, contains another splendid picture, the *Adoration of the Magi* by Martin Schwarz, 1480. Notice the hats!

Reliquary Arch
and Treasury

The visitor should then go up the short spiral staircase to the **Reliquary Arch and Treasury** containing cathedral treasures as well as silver lent by Norwich and Norfolk parish churches. The ceiling was painted in the thirteenth century. This Treasury, given by the Goldsmiths Company of London in 1973, was controversial. Younger members of the congregation suggested that followers of Jesus of Nazareth ought not to stress the wealth which the church has accumulated down the centuries. Agreement was reached when it was decided that all the offerings in the box at the foot of the stairs, at present amounting to about £3,000 a year, donated by visitors to the Treasury, should go to Christian Aid so that the treasures of the past could assist the under-privileged of today. The gift is handed over each year at the Advent Carol Service to the Norwich Chairman of Christian Aid to inaugurate their Christmas Appeal.

After leaving the Treasury the visitor will notice the Erpingham window, a fine collection of fragments of medieval glass arranged by Dennis King, the contemporary Norwich glazier.

The Cloisters

The cloisters are the largest in any English cathedral, erected after the Norman cloisters had been destroyed in a violent city versus cathedral riot in 1272. Enter through the Prior's Door with its seven finely carved figures. The roofs have a remarkable collection of bosses, including St Christopher at the north-west corner, and at the south-west corner one of the first representations of a windmill, with the miller.

Many of the 400 bosses illustrate the dark side of the medieval subconscious, the nightmares of dangerous and frightening times, as well as the weird stories of the apocalypse, indicating the immense range of human experience to be discovered in cathedrals. Two of the bosses in the east walk deserve special attention: St John and the eagle, and the happy musicians.

Notice also the monk's **lavatorium** (washing place) at the south-west corner, the coats of arms of those who dined with Queen Elizabeth I in 1578 (north wall), and the coats of arms of Archbishop Matthew Parker, the Norfolk man who played a shrewd and mediating role in recreating the Church of England under Elizabeth I (north-west corner). The open

 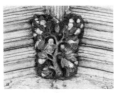

Two roof bosses, Magdalen recognising Christ and Owl in a Pear Tree

grass of the cloisters, which is used for social gatherings, madrigals, and many other events, gives a splendid view of the tower and spire by day or floodlit at night.

The cloisters also give access to a new door in the south-west corner, leading to the car park, available to visitors and worshippers on Saturdays and Sundays.

The Close

The Close is one of the largest and most charming collections of cathedral houses surviving in Europe, and covers the area occupied by the monastic buildings. It has the friendly atmosphere of a small but busy village – more an 'Open' than a Close. In the Upper Close are statues of Nelson and Wellington. The finest view of the cathedral tower and spire can be seen by walking through the Close to the River Wensum at Pull's Ferry and then going along the Riverside Walk between the Wensum and the school playing field.

The Close contains about eighty houses, twelve of them accommodating cathedral staff, Norwich School with its classrooms, playing fields and boarding houses, the diocesan headquarters, and the office of the Friends at 73 The Close (open during office hours for those who wish to join the Friends). The Close is administered by the Steward to the Dean and Chapter in co-operation with the city authorities. The Chapter Clerk, a solicitor, the Financial Agent, an accountant, the Architect, the Organist, the Precentor, the Sacrist and the Secretary of the Friends all meet frequently with the Dean and the three Residentiary Canons to ensure sensitive planning and administration.

The Dean and Chapter still carry ultimate authority for the Close, and act as trustees for the whole community. The revenues are used for the upkeep of the cathedral.

The Close was not planned but has developed down the centuries. It provides an essential background to the cathedral. No one building is of outstanding architectural merit, but as a whole the Close is most attractive. Only twelve houses out of eighty have been allowed to become offices, and car parking is controlled. Volunteers have recently planted thousands of daffodils. It is a village within a city providing a rich and varied texture of life, attitudes and abilities. Here over the years you may discover men and women with every type of job and background.

Here too was a meadow formerly leased to Sir Thomas Browne, the Norwich doctor (1605–82), and author of *Religio Medici*, whose concern was to reconcile religion and science. 'Surely', he said, 'there is a piece of divinity in us, something which was before the elements and owes no allegiance unto the sun.' Here is the Deanery, now divided into four houses,

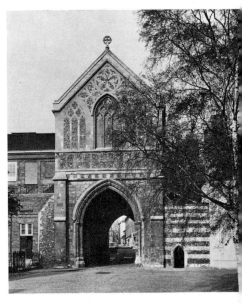

formerly the home of the priors and so one of the oldest inhabited houses in Norwich. It contains the thirteenth-century Priors' Hall. Something of St Benedict's intentions survives in the Close – a community which aims at being tolerant, humane and unobtrusively serviceable. St Benedict and Losinga would have been startled by the babies in their prams – for there are young families as well as retired people – but would have rejoiced at the community spirit with all its sharing of joys and sorrows and tasks.

Left Erpingham Gate

Right St Ethelbert's Gate

The Visitors' Centre

The Visitors' Centre over the cloisters has a model of the medieval monastery and surroundings, as well as of the ships which brought the stone from Caen. Medieval paintings, seals, stained glass, manuscripts and alabaster are all on view. The exhibition, entitled **Vision of God, a Search for Meaning**, traces the religious and philosophical ideas behind the development of the Christian faith. Concluding sections deal with the problems and possibilities of faith in the modern world, where so often it appears that God is dead. The problems posed by scientific discovery for traditional views of religion, as well as the theories of Darwin, Marx and Freud, are objectively discussed. The final section on the search for God in the world today is dominated by strong black and white photographs of moments of joy in life in Norfolk and England as well as by the heroic figure of Mother Teresa at work in Calcutta. There is also a slide/tape theatre. Children enjoy the models and the slides which alert them to the hidden treasures and details of the cathedral. Enter up the staircase at the west end of the cathedral. Here too are the cloisters' coffee room, shop and toilets.

Various Activities

The Cathedral congregation have special links with many outside communities, including the Norwich Night Shelter (for the homeless), the Taizé Ecumenical Community in France, the German Roman Catholic Parish of Ahlen, and Christian Aid. Lay committees work with the Dean and Chapter to co-ordinate worship and life at the Cathedral. Theological discussions, seminars and Bible study are organised from time to time.

Publications
and Acknowledgements

Other publications are the Cotman guide *Norwich Cathedral*, Alan B. Webster, MA, BD, *Norwich Cathedral Bosses & Misericords*, Arthur Whittingham, MA, FSA, RIBA.

Gilbert Thurlow, formerly Vice-Dean of this cathedral, Ian Dunn, Arthur Whittingham, Eric Fernie and John Mills have helped me from their continuing research. I also thank Mrs Jean Bean, the cathedral secretary, for her willing helpfulness. To keep in touch with the cathedral, a visitor can be sent by post the programmes of the Cathedral Recitals Society, the Friends, special events, and the Cathedral Newsletter (published monthly). The cathedral congregation, whose representative consultation meets regularly to discuss its worship and life, can be contacted through the joint secretaries, c/o the Cathedral Office.

The *Eastern Daily Press* publishes every morning details of the music sung at the cathedral. The Cathedral Office (telephone 20715) is always glad to answer questions about the current work of the cathedral. Coloured slides, recordings by the choir and a wide variety of published guides are available at the shop. Young people's groups and visiting choirs are specially welcome. Clergy and ministers who wish to take part in worship will be very welcome in the vestry.

Worship at the Cathedral

Services Daily:	7.35 a.m.	Mattins
	8.00 a.m.	Holy Communion
	5.15 p.m.	Evensong (3.30 p.m. or 5.15 p.m. on Saturdays), also Holy Communion 11.00 a.m. Tuesdays and Thursdays
	12.30 p.m.	Wednesdays and Fridays
Sunday:	7.35 a.m.	Mattins
	8.00 a.m.	Holy Communion
	11.00 a.m.	Holy Eucharist
	3.30 p.m.	Evensong
	7.00 p.m.	Informal Service

The cathedral uses the A.S.B. and 1662 Holy Communion Services. Communicant members of all churches are welcome to make their communion. Special arrangements for services for visiting groups of all denomnations can be made if application is made in advance to the Cathedral Office.

Right: Norwich Cathedral from the south-east; the grave of Edith Cavell; the Dean in the visitors' centre. *Back cover:* Part of Despenser Reredos (*see page 23*).

ISBN 0–7117–0142–3

©1984 Printed in Great Britain by Jarrold & Sons Ltd, Norwich. 384